There was a sad boy from Guyana

He'd woken up in his nirvana

There was a sad puggle from Belize

and finished it all with a sneeze

There was a small emu from Chile

_ _

_ _

_ _

and said "ooh the metal's quite chilly"

There was a fat squirrel from Beirut

----

and tripped and fell down the trash chute

There was a huge mouse from Barbados

---

and everything fell into chaos

There was a blue prince from Burundi

----

and didn't sleep any 'til Sunday

There was a huge boa from China

in his past life he was a miner

There was a brave wren from Croatia

----

in make up that looked like a geisha

There was a mad roach from Colombo

---

and ordered his meal as a Jumbo

There was a plump muskox from Cairo

----

and colored it in with a biro

There was a quaint ray from Astana

while endlessly seeking nirvana

There was a quaint deer from Andorra

---

and got a namedrop in the Torah

There was a sad eagle from Bahrain

and left all their socks on a train

There was a sad jaguar from Berlin

And chose to keep living in sin

There was an ill toucan from Belgrade

- -

- -

- -

and slipped by with a passing grade

There was a kind mite from Abuja

- -

- -

- -

and said that they thought that they knew ya

There was a short lady from Georgia

And then he became an explorer

There was a small wombat from Brussels

occasionally flexing his muscles

There was a brave marmot from Cyprus

all because a bit of old bike rust

There was an old lion from Djibouti

---

that looked a lot like a big ruby

There was a small stork from Botswana

And cooked it into a lasagna

There was a fat otter from Amman

which then sparked a city-wide ban

There was a scared bee from Angola

----

and got diagnosed as bipolar

There was a mad hedgehog from Cuba

‑ ‑

‑ ‑

‑ ‑

And swole to the size of a buddha

There was a bald dolphin from Bangkok

---

and kept it all in their left sock

There was a bored titmouse from Banjul

and knitted a new one with wool

There was a fun raven from Baghdad

----

before they became a grandad

There was an odd jackal from Brazil

_____

_____

_____

And some say he's doing it still

There was a young peacock from Finland

- -

- -

- -

until a storm forced the boat inland

There was a tall wombat from Beijing

----

but luckily it didn't sting

There was a mean penguin from Brunei

Until he got poked in the eye

There was a fit jaguar from Dhaka

Which he fed to his pet alpaca

There was a drab bullfrog from Dakar

- -

- -

- -

all covered in oil and tar

There was an old bee from Cape Verde

----

a fact that he heard from a birdie

There was an old man from Asmara

- -

- -

- -

and covered their face in mascara

There was a fun squirrel from Ghana

- -

- -

- -

and yelled "No one move, or I'll harm her"

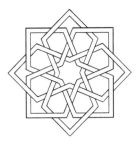

There was a rogue ostrich from Algiers

----

and ended up switching careers

There was a tall tuna from Guinea

a pig that was rather quite skinny

There was a kind muskox from Denmark

and next to his name was a checkmark

There was a green panther from Bishkek

But didn't know how to speak Czech

There was a shy zebra from Cape Town

_____

_____

_____

and did it all wearing a crown

There was an old dog from Caracas

‑‑ ‑‑

‑‑ ‑‑ ‑‑ ‑‑ ‑‑ ‑‑ ‑‑ ‑‑ ‑‑ ‑‑ ‑‑ ‑‑ ‑‑ ‑‑ ‑‑ ‑‑ ‑‑ ‑‑ ‑‑ ‑‑

‑‑ ‑‑ ‑‑ ‑‑ ‑‑ ‑‑ ‑‑ ‑‑ ‑‑ ‑‑ ‑‑ ‑‑ ‑‑ ‑‑ ‑‑ ‑‑ ‑‑ ‑‑ ‑‑ ‑‑

and ran off to be in the circus

There was an ill leopard from Benin

All done with his best gangsta' lean

There was a fun king from Grenada

- -

- -

- -

exclaimed, "can it get any harder?!"

There was a fit tick from Ankara

---

adopting a pet capybara

There was a cool bullfrog from Bissau

But didn't dare ask the man how

There was a tall takin from Bhutan

and bellowed "I AM BUT A MAN!"

There was a short raccoon from Haiti

A rather nice and rich Kuwaiti

There was a small hedgehog from Dublin

They found it later in a dustbin

There was a dumb bongo from Fiji

----

but found the job to be quite easy

CPSIA information can be obtained
at www.ICGtesting.com
Printed in the USA
LVHW082129280321
682767LV00035B/2009